Dream

Think

&

Live Big

Wire Your Mind to Conquer Adversity, Overcome Resistance, Achieve True Success, and Unleash Your Inner-Creative Genius.

About the Author

Stellan Moreira is young and motivated entrepreneur and best-selling author on a mission to change himself, and the world.

While he may be young, his information is valuable. He is self-educated, and he plans on instilling a certain sense of understanding within each reader that he has been fortunate to be able to instill within himself. This understanding has allowed him to accomplish so much, and keeps him constantly looking forward with gratitude, understanding, and determination to reach all his goals. Not only this, but it has allowed him to truly understand himself, and find a beautiful sense of peace and happiness he has always longed for. From this point onward, he realized that we wanted and needed to share his values, thoughts, information, and beliefs with the rest of the world. He realized that each individual has a meaningful purpose, and he put it upon himself to place great effort towards helping as many people find and realize their own.

His sincere mission and purpose is to help as much as he possibly can. He wants you to do the best in everything, and he wants you to succeed. What most people don't realize is that they already possess all the powers needed to make their lives completely filled with happiness, peace, wealth, and abundance, and the only thing truly standing in their way is themselves: the limiting thoughts and beliefs that they harbor in their minds. These beliefs tell them that they can't accomplish their dreams, that they can't be happy, and that they can't live the life they wish they were meant for. He is here to tell you right now that these thoughts are beyond untrue. They are so false, and yet we constantly allow them to successfully blind each and every one of us from our true potential.

Stellan is here to completely change this. He is here to make a difference in each and every readers lives.

He will never stop, for this is only the beginning.

The power of the mind is limitless; utilize it, and live a life beyond worth living.

- Stellan Moreira

This book is dedicated to family: we

love you, and appreciate everything

you have done for us. For without you,

we would be nothing.

I love you bayboo: forever and always.

Thank you.

**Follow the Author
@StellanMoreira and
@MissionFreedom for book
updates & free offers, inspiring
content, motivational stories,
and other resources to help you
wire your "growth" mentality,
achieve profound success, and
*"live a life beyond worth living."***

**MissionFreedom
StellanMoreira**

StellanMoreira

**MissionFreedom
StellanMoreira**

Dream, Think, & Live Big

By

Stellan Moreira

Introduction

Thank you for taking the time to read this. This book is filled with the proper information, motivation, and guidance that will not only allow you, but push you towards completely changing the current state of your life for the better. Not only this, but this book will aid you in realizing your full, unlimited potential, which will allow you to unleash your creative genius, become the best version of yourself, and construct the life of your dreams.

*"I swing **big**, with everything I've got. I hit **big** or I miss **big**. I like to live as **big** as I can." – Babe Ruth*

This is a book of inspiration. Without a doubt, we all need a powerful source of motivation to help us through this relatively difficult life. We all face different circumstances, but for a lot of us, success hasn't been the easiest thing to achieve. We all want more happiness; We all want good relationships; We all want more money. But how do we change the current direction of our life, so that at the end of it all, we have achieved what we've wanted, and we have everything we could have ever dreamed of?

It all starts with a single moment; a moment where we realize how truly blessed we are just to be humans. A moment where we finally understand how capable we are of achieving absolutely ANYTHING that comes to our minds. A moment where we realize that this world is ours for the taking; we can personalize it, we can change it, and we can add to it. We can create anything; for we are humans: beings with unlimited mental potential, with the ability to make the world a completely different place tomorrow from what it is today. Beings with the capability to live life exactly how we want to live it. This is who we are, and we must come to grips with the fact that life doesn't have to be hard, it doesn't have to be sad, and it doesn't have to be unfulfilling. We can make it however want. All it takes is the power to turn the switch; All it takes is the **willingness**, the **desire** to understand where we are, where want to go, and the actions we must begin taking to get there.

So in truth, there's only one question to ask before you continue reading this book.

Can you do it? Or more so, are you **willing** to do it?

*So, if you want to change your life, **continue reading this book**. If you want to learn how to switch your mindset with ease, and live the life you have always dreamed of living, **continue reading***

this book. *If you want to get the most out of your day, and squeeze every little drop of opportunity out of life,* **continue reading this book**.

Have you ever considered the idea that although we all live different lives, face different situations, and live through different experiences we are, at our core, the same? One soul separated into different beings, experiencing itself subjectively.

The Germans have a word for the feeling of realizing in an instant that the billions of people who live across this world all live a life as varied, complex, and difficult as your own; *sonder*.

It's obvious when you think about it; everyone leads a life filled with struggles, victories, sin and virtue. Yet despite all these differences we have far more in common than we let ourselves believe. Within reason, we all have the same bodies and minds, the same genetic structure. The same ten fingers and ten toes. We all experience a childhood and face different situations; bullies, test results, parents, a favorite toy. In other words, we may grow in different directions, but we come from the same root.

If then, a human can stand on the moon, beat the market, build a life filled with happiness and abundance, become top of their field, or be exemplary leaders, teachers, scientists, motivators, artists or even gardeners, then why can't you?

Does it occur to you that each of us has a significant, unique, and powerful potential within ourselves? You have control over your demise and control over your success.

A wise man will acknowledge that there are forces *mostly* outside of his control (the behavior of other people, politics, whether or not your car breaks down). He will not blame the external world for his circumstances. He will realize that there are always actions or preparations he can take to affect those things that are mostly outside of his control. If there is truly nothing he can do then he is best served by focusing his attention on those things he can change. This is the what some people call *flow*, a state wherein your direction and tranquility is mostly uninterrupted by external events. In this state of flow, one expresses oneself in perfect alignment with one's goals and ambitions, externalities do not interrupt the flow because they are not resisted, but accepted.

When successful people talk about how they became so successful, they inevitably talk about their upbringing: the experiences that molded them, the situations that taught them, and the opportunities that made them. But these successful people come from a dizzying array of backgrounds; rich and poor, smart and slow, no family or strong family. While these variables must no doubt impact people, the curious thing is that these successful people all share one thing: a determined mindset. They don't rely on fickle motivation or luck. They work hard, they pay attention, they alter their internal beliefs based on evidence, they are willing to change and be changed.

But most of all they are determined.

Most people are both their own problem and their own solution. People may claim "oh but I'm different, I have X problem, or Y problem." but if that's truly what's holding them back then why are there so many people in this world that have faced tougher situations, more adversity, yet were able to come out on top and become leaders, creators and some of the most awesome (in the old sense of the word) people this world has ever seen? Oprah Winfrey. Gary Vaynerchuk. John Paul Dejoria. Richard Branson. Sylvester Stallone. All these people faced terrible adversity; homelessness, hunger, rejection from loved ones, and many went broke ***more than once***. Yet, somehow, they still came out on top. They still became who they wanted to be: the person they believed they were destined to become.

Why are there so many people, some who even by modern standards live a privileged existence, who can't achieve the life of their dreams?

Is it because they haven't been punched in the mouth hard enough to understand what true adversity is?

You're close to the truth.

If someone doesn't face enough challenges in their life, if they have it easy, are never forced to really strive, or grow, then they will not have developed the **mindset** that is necessary to succeed without luck.

The main reason the examples above accomplished what they did is this: they believed in themselves. They told themselves that they could create something truly beautiful and significant, **so they did**. They told themselves that they *can* live the life they felt in their heart they were meant for, **so they did**. They told themselves that they were the sole determinants of the reality they live, so they took the leap forward and began creating their destiny from scratch. Not only this, but they knew what they wanted, and they knew that no one on the face of this planet was going to give it to them. Therefore, they had only one option: to work, hustle, and grind each and every day until they made it. And this is precisely what they did.

They believed in themselves so entirely they placed their heart and soul into every venture. They kept in mind an idea: "If someone else has done it, I can do it too."

More than that, they *acted* on their belief. They made sacrifices for their future. Belief is nothing without action, as we'll find out later.

As the founder of Dropbox, Drew Houston famously said; "The most successful people I know are obsessed with solving an important problem, something that matters to them. They remind me of a dog chasing a tennis ball: Their eyes go a little crazy, the leash snaps and they go bounding off, plowing through whatever gets in the way."

What's important, says Drew, is finding your own tennis ball.

By reading this book you have taken the first step to finding that ball; you've preselected yourself for a better future. One that will accomplish your dreams, expand your thinking and allow you to create the life you desire: **the life of your dreams**.

Welcome to Dream, Think, and Live Big.

Part 1

DREAM

'Begin with the End in Mind'

The first part of the mindset of success (or flow) is *dreaming.*

In other words, to *"begin with the end in mind."*

At the most basic level, to "begin with the end in mind" is to begin today with the vision, image, and perception of the end of your life as your frame of reference or criterion by which everything else is examined and perceived. Each part of your life – yesterday's words, today's behavior, tomorrow's actions – should be examined according to the "whole": the general purpose and intention of your desires, of what truly matters to you. By sustaining the "end" – the overall goal you wish to achieve – in your mind, you live each moment, each day, each second in a meaningful way that contributes to the vision you have of your life as whole.

To *begin with the end in mind* simply means to proceed with a clear understanding of the destination, or goal you wish to achieve. In other words, it means to know where you are going so that you better understand where you currently are and the steps you need to take to begin heading in the right direction: the path that leads you to the achievement, fulfillment, success, and happiness **you** genuinely desire.

In truth, it is beyond easy to get caught up in the busyness of life; to place extreme effort towards climbing the ladder of success only to figure out, towards the end of it all, that you've been climbing the wrong ladder. Therefore, it's incredibly easy to be busy without being effective; without placing effort towards climbing the ladder of success that links with our passions, the things that will allow us to feel fulfilled.

Without a doubt, it is extremely common for people to find themselves achieving empty victories; achievements and accomplishments that don't align with their inner-values and beliefs, and ones that may have come at the expense of things they suddenly realize were far more valuable to them.

Little do we know how radically different our realities could be if we simply just understood the true importance's of our lives. When we keep those picture's in our mind, we live each day and manage ourselves according to the things that matter most to us: the values and beliefs that are directly aligned with our inner-most genuine desires and passions. If we keep climbing the wrong ladder, each and every step we take just gets us to the wrong place faster. We may be extremely busy; we may be placing greater effort in climbing this ladder than we ever have, and shedding blood, sweat, and tears all along the way, we may be very *efficient,* but until we begin with the end in mind, we will never be truly *effective.*

Here's a perfect example.

Back in the 70's a young man named Sylvester Stallone was broke, homeless, and sleeping in a bus shelter in LA with only his pet dog for company. He had a clear vision though. In his bag was a script, one that he had painstakingly written and revised. One that he was fiercely passionate about. He'd received rejection after rejection from studios and was down to his last few dimes. The next day he had a meeting with Universal. They loved the script and wanted it desperately. But Stallone had one stipulation; he had to be the star of the film. Shocked at the demand the studio refused to put an unknown as the lead in a movie, and Stallone declined their offer.

The next day, hungry and broke, Stallone sold his dog in order to make ends meet a little longer on the streets. He was *determined* to succeed. A few days later he met with MGM. They loved the story, and agreed to let him star in the film. *Rocky* came out in 76' and was an instant success, launching Sylvester Stallone's career as one of the most famous action heroes the world has ever seen.

He bought his dog back a few days later.

As you can see, this man dreamt. He saw the goals he wanted to achieve in his mind, and fell so deeply in love with them that he never stopped until he accomplished them. He did everything and anything in his power to acquire the role for the film, and although he was constantly rejected, his self-belief kept driving him forward. He never, not even for a second, stopped believing in himself or his dreams. He never told himself: "Everyone keeps rejecting me, I should just stop trying. I should just give up." Instead, he told himself: "I will never stop trying. I have one life, and I will do everything in my power to be able to live it the way I want. I will achieve my dreams. I just have to keep moving forward." And this is exactly what he did. Similar to a great majority of accomplished people, Sylvester Stallone knew there was no other option for his life other than to succeed in his passion. He knew that the law of averages was on his side, and he knew that if he kept trying, he would receive the opportunity he had always dreamed of receiving, at least once.

As people with dreams; As people with passions, and genuine aspirations, we must believe in ourselves, and we must strive to achieve what our heart genuinely desires. We must understand that, as humans, we our beyond powerful. We have so much potential within us, yet we constantly allow ourselves remain blind to the fact that we CAN achieve; that we CAN live the life we desperately wish we were meant for.

We must remove these self-blinding beliefs COMPLETELY from our lives. We must fill our hearts and minds with thoughts and beliefs that push us to achieve, that push us to live, that push us, with a fiery passion, to pursue the reality we have always envisioned in our minds.

You have a beautiful, amazing, and extraordinary mind; this is the same for everyone. All of us have the capability to think, and the thoughts we nurture and support shape the **entire course of our life**.

Do you ever wonder why so many accomplished people like Tony Robbins, Jim Carrey, Steve Jobs, and Warren Buffet achieved incredible amount of fame, wealth, and abundance, despite having experienced extreme poverty, hardships, and obstacles? While you may think it was because the universe was kinder to them, this is not true. The truth is that all these people achieved everything they dreamt of because of the positive and unlimited thoughts they harbored and nurtured in their minds. They told themselves that they could create something truly beautiful and significant, **so they did**. They told themselves that they can accomplish anything they placed their mind and heart on, **so they did**. They told themselves that they are **unlimited in every single way possible,** so they took the leap forward, and began creating their destiny from scratch.

This goes for anyone that has ever achieved profound success in absolutely anything; if you have ever found yourself envying a friend who started small and was not as stable as you were at a time, but is now living a wonderful and fulfilled life, this is also because of the sort of beliefs that friend supported.

Suppose your friend is a "he".

Your friend believed in himself. Your friend nurtured his mind with a constant supply of positive thoughts that, overtime, turned into strong, healthy beliefs that completely changed and improved his life for the better. Your friend chose to believe in the things he wanted to manifest in his life, and that is exactly what he did. As Karen Marie Moning said, *"what you choose to believe makes you the person you are."*

If you are not proud of yourself and the kind of life you have built so far, lay the blame on your thoughts and beliefs. Fortunately, however, by changing your thoughts and beliefs, you can change the entire course of your life. You can make your life brighter, better, more beautiful, and more meaningful than it has ever been before: all you must do is **believe**.

If you want abundance, you **can** accomplish that. If you want heaps of wealth, you **can** actualize that. Happiness, good health, spirituality, love, healthy relationships, an attractive physique, and all the riches in life: all these things can be yours, but **only** if you nurture the right thoughts, and transform them into powerful beliefs you will live by for the rest of your life.

Chapter 1

Visualization

If you don't know where you're going, you'll almost certainly never get there. Visualization is a vital component of the success mindset, it's important to periodically imagine yourself at the position in life that you want to be in so that you may check your direction and change course if necessary. A powerful goal is an anchor that can keep you steady you in times of trouble or weakness. Life will sometimes catch us off-guard, and if we don't have our purpose or goal clearly fixated in our minds, we'll be thrown off our current "path", and placed on a new one. Try the exercise below to find your life-goal.

Exercise

Let's try an exercise. Close your eyes and visualize the person you want to become, see that image as a separate person, standing right in front of you. This person is the ultimate you – the version of yourself you long to become.

Ask yourself some questions: What qualities or traits does this person have that I don't?

What type of relationships does this person have that I don't?

What kind of values does this person embody? Are they the same as mine now?

Does this idealized version of you stand by their values?

What has this person achieved? What impacts have they made on themselves and those around him?

Negative Visualization Exercise

Imagine where your current actions might lead. Are you working hard enough? Are you spending time pursuing your dream every day? Be radically honest with yourself; are you on track?

Picture what your career might be like if you waste the now. Will you accomplish that goal without hard work? Will you have that house, partner, business, or lifestyle you dream of? Can you really afford that day, week, month where you're not pursuing your target? How will you feel if you fall just short of success?

Picture your lifestyle at 70 if you continue to neglect your health now. Infirm, forgetful, incontinent. How much will you long for the strength and vitality of your youth? What will you regret not having done? What will you regret doing?

Remind yourself that truly the only limited resource we have on this planet is time.

If we misspend it there are no refunds.

What you should feel if you're off-track is <u>intensely uncomfortable</u> with these thoughts. This is good. It's a warning signal from your ego, telling you not to look too closely at the difference between your goals and reality. Your ego is warning you because it's afraid, but thank it instead, and delve into the problem.

Remind yourself that if the mere *idea* is this bad then *living* with missed opportunities or poor health will be far worse. Face this fear, plan and take steps to ensure you've done everything in your power to make your dreams a reality.

Don't live a life with regrets.

Remember: The biggest regrets we will ever have are not the things we have done, but the things we did not do: the book we never wrote, the world-wide expeditions we never took, the business we never started.

Stop thinking, stop procrastinating, and stop excusing; Just start doing.

Chapter 2

Affirmation

Affirmations are phrases and statements you repeatedly say to yourself to speak a certain belief into your life. These self-proclaimed suggestions can be neutral, positive, or negative, and when you frequently say them to yourself, your subconscious begins to accept them as your own. Once your subconscious mind accepts something, the suggestion imbeds itself into your neural pathway and begins shaping your thinking. Affirmations work in a similar manner as your thoughts: **they influence your subconscious mind to shape your beliefs.**

This means that if you frequently say positive things to yourself and tell yourself you can achieve something, you will eventually start to **genuinely** believe it. These positive thoughts will attract great opportunities and experiences towards you, and will allow you to truly prosper and succeed.

Even with a clear goal, sometimes the many obstacles and challenges life randomly throws in our direction will get in the way. You may begin to stray off the course of your intended purpose and begin listing on the winds of chance, focusing and going towards nothing in particular. Which is why affirmations are so important: we can use them to remind ourselves of where we're going, and the intention and purpose behind the path were on.

If you turn practicing positive affirmations into an everyday habit, you will strengthen your self-belief, develop an attitude that is friendly to the pursuit of your dreams, and build an empowered life. You will stop settling for the mediocre, and instead settle for nothing less than what adds actual value to your life. This will ultimately help you cultivate the life of your **dreams**.

Next...

Now that you understand the power of affirmations, here is what you need to do to practice them regularly:

Remember: When you create an affirmation, ensure that you are following the three P's;

- Present
- Personal
- Positive

1 Think of anything you want to change in yourself, any area you want to improve at, or any goal you want to achieve.

2 Write down that thing or goal and then build a positive and present-oriented affirmation around it. Positive here means your affirmation should not include words that have a negative connotation; words such as 'not, never, and 'cannot.' Your subconscious does not recognize the word "not". When you use the phrase in an affirmation, the mind changes the suggestion accordingly. For instance, if you said, "I am not going to be sad," your subconscious mind will change the affirmation to "I am going to be sad." Rather than using negative words in your suggestions, **focus on positive words**. If you wish to be happy, say, "I am happy." Further, the affirmation must be present-focused which means it should make you feel as if you have already achieved your intention. For instance, to attract abundance into your life, say, "I am enjoying great abundance in my life" instead of saying "I want to live a life full of abundance." When you say the latter or any affirmation focused on the future, an affirmation such as "I am going to work hard" or "I am going to be successful," your thoughts will focus on the future and your present will remain devoid of that blessing or goal. As you create affirmations, create positive and present-oriented affirmations.

3 Keep your affirmation as clear and concise as possible. An affirmation of 20 to 30 words is ok, but it is best to keep your affirmation about seven to ten words long. Shorter affirmations are easier to speak, recall, and you can easily repeat them.

4 After crafting your affirmation, write it down in your journal and chant it aloud for about 10 to 20 minutes. To improve its effectiveness, write down the affirmation as you speak it.

5 Speak each word loudly and clearly. Emphasize important words in the affirmation. If an affirmation

reads "I breathe in confidence and exhale stress," then emphasize **breathe in**, **confidence**, **exhale**, and **stress**.

6 Feel what you say. If you say, "I am happy," actually smile and inject your maximum belief into the suggestion. The more you believe what you say, the stronger it will affect your mind; when you truly believe something, you become ready act upon that belief. To understand this effect, say "I am happy" twice. In the first instance, say it half-heartedly, then repeat the same statement with complete belief, and as you do it, put a big grin on your face. Compare the feelings you experience the second time with those you experience the first time. You will notice a remarkable difference in how you feel now. You will truly start to feel good and happy inside. **This is the power of belief**.

7 Truly visualize yourself achieving the goal you just set. If you are saying, "I am happy," imagine yourself being the happiest person in the world and feeling that the whole world belongs to you. If you are saying, "I am successful and wealthy," envision being the most prosperous person in the world and living a life filled with nothing other than success and abundance. Live each moment of your visualization and you will start to feel what you say. The practice of combining belief and positive affirmations and then visualizing them turns the affirmation into an incantation. Incantations are a practice Tony Robbins, world-renowned self-help author and coach, swears by. An incantation is simply an empowering suggestion you give to yourself to improve your mentality.

8 Keep practicing this for 10 to 20 minutes or more. For best results, do it twice a day.

9 For even better results, do it once immediately after waking up and then before going to bed. When you say empowering things to yourself when you rise, you set a positive basis for your day. Secondly, by repeating those or similar suggestions before going to bed, you give yourself positive mental food to linger in your mind while you sleep. This will place your mind in a certain state, allowing you to wake up in the mood your suggestion promotes.

Chapter 3

Personal Mission Statement

As Lewis Carroll, author of *Alice In Wonderland* once said:

> *"If you don't know where you're going, any road will get you there."*

Don't you have somewhere to be? Some place and time in life that excites you and fills you with a nervous trepidation? If not, don't you have something you'd like to *avoid*?

A personal mission statement can help us do all that and more. A PMS will;

- Provide a focus and direction for your life
- Reinforce your intentions
- Simplify your decision making
- Hold you accountable for any decisions you do make

Exercise

I keep six honest serving-men

(They taught me all I knew);
Their names are What and Why and When
*And How and Where and Who - **Rudyard***
Kipling

What:

What do you want from life, what do you care about? Make it bigger-than-big, the more passionate you are, the better.

E.g. I want to be the most successful accountant the world has ever seen.

Why:

Now ask yourself the why. Why do you want this? Why do you want it so much. Try and find a reason that doesn't rely on weak motivators like the respect of others or fame.

E.g. Because nothing gives me more happiness than working with numbers.

How:

How will you accomplish this thing? How can you phrase it in a single sentence? Consider your what and why answers now. How can this form a single direction, a single statement?

E.g. Math and work will always come first above play and laziness.

Make sure to go in depth.

Part 2

THINK

The Ego and the Self

When considering the way we approach our lives, one paradigm that is particularly useful is the idea of the Ego and the Self. In this idea, the Ego represents "I", an internal state in which our focus and practices are guided by our wants, desires and impulses.

The Self represents "We"; an external state that considers others, the needs of humanity as a whole. It broadens the perspective and smoothens the path of life. When we are in Ego mode, a personal insult from a colleague may cause a painful dissonance between your idea of yourself and what was just said. You might react in a number of different ways; anger, sadness, laughter, bitterness.

When one is in the **Self** mode however, you will consider the larger scheme of things, that perhaps this person has their own demons with which they are struggling, that perhaps the insult is more of a reflection of them than you. That, even if these things are not true, the only way an insult can hurt you is if you agree with what was said in some way, and if this is the case and you respect the person from which the insult came, you would do well to consider what was said. If however, you do not respect the person, then why does their opinion matter so much to you?

"Remember, that what is insulting is not the person who abuses you or hits you, but [your judgment] that they are insulting."
- *Epictetus*

Chapter 4

Traits of The Selfist

Independence vs Interdependence

"The internal machinery of life, the chemistry of the parts, is something beautiful. And it turns out that all life is interconnected with all other life."
- Richard P. Feynman

Where the Ego considers only itself, the Self considers the world from a much broader perspective. An Egoist seeks independence – one's reliance on solely one's self - and they consider this to be the gold standard of living. Relying on others or even asking for help can be seen as a weakness, and so the heavy burden of "success" is lain on their shoulders alone. The word success, by its very nature, might mean "having done it on my own" to many who think from the Egoist perspective.

Those utilizing and focusing on the Selfist paradigm however, seek **interdependence**: one's reliance on one's self and those around him to create something much larger and more significant than they can create on their own. Those whose mentalities lay in the Selfist paradigm understand that forming a team and utilizing the minds of others and not just their own is a concept and practice that can and will propel one much farther down the road toward success and achievement. In other words, the greatest forms of achievement are derived from mutual dependence between ourselves, other's, and the world. This is closer to how we were designed; we are social animals after all. A Selfist recognizes that we rely on one another to greater and lesser degrees for near-everything in our lives. Even if you now live on a mountain top and speak to one person a year, you were still likely raised and educated by a society. One that clothed you, fed you, sometimes loved you and gave you life.

Chapter 5

Forgiveness

Because of this broader perspective, a Selfist will focus on forgiveness rather than anger or jealousy.

"The race is long and, in the end, it's only with yourself."
- Wear Sunscreen, Mary Schmich.

The Selfist will allow others greater quarter than he does himself. When angry about something, he will question why he has reacted this way, rather than blaming his feelings on others.

To many of us, forgiveness, whether it is forgiving those close to us or ourselves, does not come easy. Letting go of the hurt someone caused you and forgiving that person after he or she has wronged you is not as simple as it sounds. How can you compel your heart to be merciful? How can you just let go of all the anger and hate, and truly forgive?

Moreover, forgiving yourself could be just as difficult. Undoubtedly, your past is full of mistakes, and the many setbacks you experience make you feel unworthy and unhappy. When you lowly regard yourself, you will not value yourself. This will cause you to be harsh on yourself whenever you err and falter. Even worse, you will not believe in yourself. You will not supply yourself with the support you need to become the impactful, powerful, and significant person you can truly be. You must learn to forgive yourself; from there, you will let go of what was, and focus on **what can be.**

Now, in order to fully implement the habit of forgiving others and ourselves into our lives, we must first fully understand the many powerful and significant effects it has on almost every single aspect of the person we are, and the life we live.

The Powerful Effects of Forgiveness

If you are one of the few that can truly harness the power of forgiveness, your life will be whatever you want it to be. Although you may not genuinely realize it now, I can guarantee its effects will become apparent quickly. The power of forgiveness will positively impact almost all aspects of your life. Here a few examples.

Forgiveness Saves Your Time and Energy

When was the last time you were truly furious about something or someone? Recall that time, and think of how you felt. Were you seething with rage? Did you boil up and create a big scene? Did you waste a lot of time quarrelling with someone to prove your point? Did that entire scenario exhaust you? Did it leave you feeling sad for days, affect your productivity at work, your relationships at home and affect you in many other ways? If yes, then you have experienced the utter horribleness of what it is to be angry and unforgiving. Not only does it completely drain your energy, but it absolutely **wastes your time**; time that you could be using to improve and take a step forward, instead of one backwards. If you want to reach massive success in everything you do, remember this.

Practicing forgiveness will help you save time and energy. When you forgive someone immediately after he or she hurts you, you decommission the resentment factory inside you, which allows you to let go of strong negative emotions. This helps you use your time and energy to complete productive and self-constructive tasks.

At the same time, self-forgiveness ensures that you do not spend too much time loathing and hating the things you have done in the past; which will allow you to learn from all your mistakes, take them in to sincere consideration, and improve your acts in the future. Only this way will you change **yourself**, and change your **life**.

Forgiveness Means You Win

By allowing the person who has wronged you to swarm your everyday thoughts, and control your underlying emotions, you are literally allowing them to walk free with your happiness in their hands. You are giving them the opportunity to strip you of your positive emotions, and ruin your entire day, week, or month. Do not let this happen. Control yourself, control your life!

By simply speaking the words "I forgive you," and letting all of it go, you are the ultimate winner. You are reclaiming your happiness, and therefore a piece of your life.

Become the Boss of Your Life

Unleashing your temper, even if you are doing so occasionally, often births anger issues that hand over control to your emotions. This makes you behave irrationally and surrender control of your life. It can be very challenging to be successful if you have serious anger issues; no one wants to be around you to support whatever it is you are pursuing because of your regular anger outbursts.

By letting the other person or situation take the wheel of your thoughts and emotions, you surrender control of your own life. Forgiveness is the tool which allows you to regain control of that wheel. It will give you the opportunity to take charge of all your decisions, and live a beautiful life consisting of nothing other than health, wealth, love and happiness.

New Doors Will Open

Since you have completely freed yourself of the undermining power of negative thought, energy, and lack of control of your own happiness, you will be surprised to witness just how many new opportunities will begin to pop-up in to your life. But, it is not that they were created from thin air, it is that you have freed space in your mind and have regained control of your positive mentality, allowing you to truly think and notice all opportunities around you.

Even if you are unable to physically say the words "I forgive you" to the person, mentally say them to yourself. Alone, this will allow you to free yourself from negative constraint, and experience life in a more positive, and progressive manner.

It is important to find a healthy and positive balance in your life. Carrying around old baggage from someone who has wronged you is not helping you maintain that balance. Clear the space in your head and look forward to new and exciting opportunities, and most importantly, happiness.

Undoubtedly, it is clear to see that forgiveness is a crucial factor when it comes to building a positive mentality. Although this may be one of the most difficult habits to follow, it is truly one of the most important. Therefore, in order to experience greater ease in this, here is a list of guidelines that helped me in the beginning of my mental transformation. I hope it helps you as well.

Chapter 6

Gratitude

"Gratitude can transform common days into thanksgivings, turn routine jobs into joy, and change ordinary opportunities into blessings."
- William Arthur Ward

A Selfist understands that they have many things, no matter their current situation and circumstance, to be utterly grateful for: from their mobile phone, to their sight. They will actively spend time practicing gratitude for the many things life has given them. As a result, they are happier and much more willing and able to pursue their purpose, and create the life they visualize in their dreams.

Not only this, but gratitude is a tool that has allowed every successful person to succeed, every accomplished person to accomplish, and every happy person to be happy. Gratitude is a tool that we can and should utilize every day. We should be grateful for the fact that we are human: we have beautiful and powerful minds to think, arms and hands to touch and feel, and legs to move around. We have the ability to perceive, to think, to learn, to grow. We have so much potential within us, yet our lack of gratitude for those very prominent aspects is what hinders us from truly unleashing our inner-powers.

Once we begin practicing gratitude and making it a significant and genuine habit within our lives, our realities will completely change. Instead of seeing the glass half empty, we will see it half full. Instead of allowing obstacles and adversities to push us to the floor and keep us there, gratitude will allow us to unlock our resilience, get back up, and keep moving forward with genuine determination and understanding.

The Power of Gratitude

As already discussed, being grateful (gratitude) means being thankful for something. Having gratitude for yourself and your life means you acknowledge every little to big blessing and quality you have and are happy about.

By cultivating gratitude, you learn to live your life in an imoroved manner. Instead of perceiving your life as a burden, you start viewing it as a miracle; your focus shifts from everything you lack, to everything you have. This helps you become more thankful and appreciative of your loved ones, your health, your life, and your desires.

Gratitude helps you quickly acknowledge all the gifts in your life and encourages you to be kinder and compassionate towards everyone. When you practice gratitude, you start noticing the good things about your loved ones, every situation you experience, and focus more on returning the kind favor. If someone helped you out, you will not whine about how he/she could have helped you better. Instead, you will be happy that he/she helped you and you shall look for ways to return the favor to him/her.

While you're thinking that being grateful might be useless and not something that helps you become successful, you would be surprised to know that a number of accomplished people in the world swear by the importance of gratitude in their lives.

Successful people such as John Paul DeJoria, Oprah Winfrey, Timothy Ferriss, and Richard Branson are a few examples of renowned, accomplished people who consciously practice gratitude and feel indebted to this state of mind for living a healthy, happy, and content life.

To follow the footsteps of these people, you must cultivate gratitude. To do so, understand that to nurture gratitude, you do not have to practice it once or twice; instead, you need to nurture that state of mind. Yes, gratitude is a state of mind, and to live a beautiful, happy, and powerful life, you must nurture it.

Gratitude is a State of Mind

The gratitude state of mind draws upon your beliefs. To nurture gratitude, it is important that you build and then strengthen the right beliefs. To do that, you need to identify all the things you feel deeply and truly grateful for. To realize this, ask yourself "What am I thankful for?" "What makes me really happy?" "Which things/blessings add value to my life?' Ask yourself other similar questions. These questions make you more aware of your blessings and help you think positively.

When you become emotionally charged and thankful for everything you have, your emotions serve as the catalysts for extremely intense and magical transformations in your life. This transformation is often beyond everyone's imagination. While you may find this bizarre right now, ask yourself the following: do you want to live a life of abundance? Do you want to be better than you have ever been before? Do you want your wishes and desires to manifest as fast as possible? Since your answers to these questions are likely to be a 'YES,' gratitude is all you need to make it come true. Yes, like a magical elixir, gratitude does have the power to make all your wishes come true.

If someone gave you his word that if you drank a potion from a specific vial, all your dreams would become reality, you are likely to give that person your attention and drink from the vial, right? Well, gratitude is a magical potion that can do all these things for you. By simply building an appreciative mindset, you can cultivate the life you have always desired: a beautiful life you deserve to live and enjoy.

Here is how you can cultivate this state of mind.

How to Create the Gratitude State of Mind

Creating the gratitude mindset can be as complicated or as simple as you want it to be. If you are committed to becoming a thankful, kind, and humble individual who is all set to harness the power of gratitude and who is ready to pay attention to his blessings and be thankful for them, you will easily be able to do so. However, if it takes you time to settle and adjust to your current life, focus on your blessings, and let go of things you want but do not have, nurturing gratitude and harnessing its power will take time. The choice is yours and the power to do it lies within you.

Ungratefulness and gratefulness are states of your mind you nurture consciously or unconsciously. A lack of gratitude and gratitude are intangible in nature, and solely reside in your mind. The state of mind you nurture brings similar but measurable and tangible results to different aspects of your life. In other words, every thought you nurture and consistently focus on casts a certain influence on your life.

Similarly, if you nurture an ungrateful state of mind, every probability is that you are unhappy with your life. When you consistently and incessantly think that, you strengthen your ungrateful thoughts; consequently, this brings similar experiences towards you. If you keep thinking you are poor and feel unhappy about it, you will forever stay that way. Why is this so? Because when you are unhappy with your current state in life, you will always complain about it instead of looking for ways to improve it. On top of that, you will send negative, unthankful thoughts to the universe. When you send negative thoughts out into the universe, you get negative experiences in return.

On the other hand, if you choose to be grateful, you shall start focusing on all you currently have. If you do not own a big house, at least you have a small apartment, and a roof over your head. If you do not own a car, at least you have money to spend on transportation. Similarly, you shall start acknowledging all the little gifts you have. This will help you build a grateful state of mind, which as you already know, will do wonders for you.

This shows that **everything** begins with a thought in your mind. Before you can manifest anything, you must think about it, and **how** you think about it plays a monumental role in shaping your reality. You may have unconsciously developed ungratefulness:

it may have crept inside you and found an abode in your mind through different cues in your environment. To develop conscious gratefulness, you must remain consistently and consciously deliberate about it.

Since everything begins in your mind and you have complete control and choice over how to shape your life, you can consciously nurture gratitude. Small efforts consciously made will help you cultivate this beautiful state of mind, and in time, you will reap miraculous benefits.

At first, you shall not realize how amazing its power is. In the start, you will just find yourself feeling happy and mildly relaxed about everything and your life. But if you consistently keep practicing gratitude, you will bring these effects to your relationships, finances, health, profession, and every other aspect of your life.

If you are ready to make this effort, simply be more conscious of the things you have in your life. Make it a habit to look for any 3 qualities in yourself every morning and appreciate yourself for those qualities. After noticing these three things and being thankful for them, thank the universe for blessing you with such amazing strengths. This helps you become content with yourself, which in turn increases your self-esteem; allowing you to believe in yourself, and constantly perform at your peak.

Secondly, eliminate the words/ phrases such as "I do not have blessing X (name of anything you do not have)," "I cannot do this because I don't have this" and other similar phrases that show you cannot achieve your goals because you lack something.

To be thankful for your life and thus, make it better, you need to eradicate such a mentality. Consciously try doing this every time you think of something that makes you feel discontent. To replace ungratefulness with gratefulness, quickly think of any blessing you have. If you consciously do this a few times daily, you will soon nurture the habit of thinking positively and being thankful for your life. This helps you build a thankful state of mind that then helps you exploit and employ the power of gratitude.

Along with gratitude, to channelize the power of the universe towards manifesting your desires, you need forgiveness. Let us talk about it next.

Chapter 7

Resilience

Having better appreciated their good fortune, when things take a turn for the worse, Selfists are resilient. They know their strengths and weaknesses, and are better able to leverage them to their advantage. They have cultivated a strong core of belief in the Self, and may even see obstacles and challenges as opportunities to grow and learn. When they exit the other side, they reflect on how they handled situations in order to improve for the future. They consider these things from an interdependent perspective.

"Resilience is all about being able to overcome the unexpected. Sustainability is about survival. The goal of resilience is to thrive."
- Jamais Cascio

A Selfist understands resilience to be an imperative part of living an empowered life. If you are not resilient, you will not bounce back each time setbacks punch you hard in the gut. When things do not go your way, you will likely feel upset and if you lack resilience, you can fall into the trap of negative thinking. Without a doubt, I can easily say that anyone who has ever experienced great success in **anything** is resilient. For without this resilience, they would have never had the **ability** and **courage** to absorb life's punches, learn from them, and keep moving forward. In fact, they would have been punched once, and remained on the floor in a puddle of pity, negativity, and unhappiness. Therefore, success in life calls for resilience and persistence. So, if you don't have these qualities, continue reading so you can learn how to acquire them. For without them, one will never be able to experience the true and profound **success** one is capable of.

To be truly happy and pave the way for success in your life, you must develop **resilience**: the ability to fight back whenever you encounter an obstacle that knocks you down. You must never settle for the mediocre, and you must always strive for greatness.

To become resilient enough to persevere through any adversity, you need to work on **three key things**: these three things are the three habits you need to develop strength and grit.

Have a Purposeful Goal

Resilience comes easy when you know what you are striving for. To be truly gritty, it is important that you **pursue your goals**. If you do not have any goal, your life will be purposeless. Success will come by chance and you are unlikely to be swayed by anything that comes by. When you lack a sense of purpose, setbacks will easily distract you and you will take your eyes off the prize.

A purpose can be anything – cultivating spirituality, a monetary goal, striving for happiness in a relationship, or anything else you truly yearn for. On the other hand, a **sincere purpose** is one that makes you feel accomplished and happy, and one that aligns your inner-most values with your desires. To find your goal or sense of purpose, think of any area of your life you want to improve, and then find out what you truly want to achieve in that area. If you are thinking of your financial life, think of what you truly desire. Think about what you want your objective to be, and what its purpose serves. While doing that, consider your strengths and past accomplishments. This will allow you to set a personal, customized, and measureable goal.

Similarly, think of what sort of goals you want to set in terms of health, happiness, relationships, love, spirituality etc. Create many goals relating to different aspects of your life and then write them down. Regularly visit those goals so they can remain in your mind and sight. This way, you will stay focused on the bigger picture and whenever a setback in that area strikes you, it will bruise you but not throw you off balance.

Believe in Yourself Every Day

Start placing more faith in your yourself. You have already learnt how to discover your strengths and hone them, now all you must do is truly believe.

What is to believe you may ask? Well, what is to know the difference between your right hand and your left hand? What is it know that one dollar plus another dollar equals two dollars?
You may think that believing and knowing are two different things, but they truly are not.

If you believe in yourself as much as you are convinced that one plus one equals two, **you will be completely limitless.** Your life will not only become whatever you want it to be, but you will change the world.

Believe that you have the power to change not only your life, but the lives of the many that surround you. Believe that a limitation is only a limitation if you perceive it as one. If you begin to believe that, you'll start to understand the undeniable truth that there are no such things as limitations. In consequence, once you begin to truly understand that, you will become **unstoppable**.

The moment you start trusting your talents is the moment you know you have what it takes to move forward and emerge victorious even when all hell breaks loose.

From this day forward, frequently go through your achievements, and **appreciate** and **reward** yourself for your strengths. This way, you will stay confident even when adversity knocks you down.

Embrace Change

Being resilient does not just mean stubbornly holding on to what you believe in; it also means being flexible and adaptable to different circumstances. As is often the case, most adversities are not obstacles at all: **they are opportunities in disguise.** If you do not know how to embrace change, you are likely to miss an excellent opportunity only to realize your mistake later on.

Resilient people are flexible because they know the right way to react to a situation. To be truly resilient, **be flexible**. If you work on building the habits of trying new things daily and seeing the good in every situation, you will slowly nurture the habit of embracing change. This will improve your level of resilience and help you **seek opportunities**.

Work on these three keys and within a short time, your level of resilience will increase, you will become mentally stronger and happier, and you will experience the massive success that can only be experienced by a small group of people: **those who create the right change.**

Chapter 8

Opportunity

"Opportunity is missed by most people because it is dressed in overalls and looks like work." -
Thomas Edison

A Selfist is constantly seeking new opportunities. They utilize the endless power of gratitude to seek the good from every situation, whether it be good, bad, or neutral. This allows them to dive deeper into the experiences they face, and derive any possible knowledge and emotional tools that will push them closer towards achieving whatever it is they wish to achieve. Not only this, but a Selfist is also constantly on the search for any new opportunity that will allow them to expand their mind and challenge their perspective.

A Selfist places great and powerful belief behind the perspective and mindset they follow, but they also understand that they are not perfect, and their mission is to consistently and persistently seek knowledge and understanding from the many mental view-points of others. This does not mean they will automatically accept the beliefs of others to be their own, but it doesn't mean they will automatically reject them either: they will juggle them around in their minds, ponder on their many aspects, and derive from them any useful information and knowledge that corresponds with the belief system they already have in place. This allows them to strengthen their mental resources, the powerful beliefs and attitudes that propel them toward action, and will truly allow them to achieve much greater success at the end of their journey.

Chapter 9

Creativity for the Self

When we cast down the walls of selfishness and look beyond ourselves to the world outside our own skin - things look clearer. Trouble and discord occur in all walks of life, we can see other people's needs and think beyond them. We can see the preciousness of existence; that if there is anything worth doing it's worth doing right, including living. Especially living.

A Selfist tries to look at themselves objectively. If there is want in their souls, merit unmet, opportunities discarded, or potential unreached they will see it. A Selfist won't try and flee from this feeling of unease at seeing the malformations of their life, instead they will seek to correct them. To tap the untapped potential of their existence and achieve the standard to which they know they should be living. After all, we don't have much time and if we are to live well, we must *act*.

Therefore a Selfist will continually seek to manifest themselves. To become who they ought to be.

Chapter 10

Manifest the Self

Whether they are a carpenter, a writer, a nurse, a bricklayer, a firefighter, or an entrepreneur, a Selfist will recognize his or her craft to be an art. In some cases, like with the writer or the painter this can be taken literally, in others like the firefighter or the brick layer it's a little different.

A Selfist understands that whatever their craft they must see it as an art in order to fully commit their creative attention and potential to it. If you are a bricklayer, you must see each wall you build as a testament to your creative character. Your ability to think around obstacles, continue despite the odds being set against you, and work hard is what will determine your success, no matter the occupation. This is how you rise above the average and stand out in your career of choice. Passion and dedication as though each brick laid were a brush stroke on the Mona Lisa.

Two types of thinking are necessary in order to achieve this state of creativity; convergence and divergence.

Convergence

Convergent thinking is the ability to use logical thinking to evaluate and critique ideas with the goal of finding the best suited solution for a given situation or criteria.

We use this type of decision making when we have all the facts at-hand and can examine a wide array of information. From here we are able to make an informed decision. We're listening to other people's opinions and weighing up the information.

Divergence

If convergent thinking is an orderly, well paced and structured process, divergent thinking is a free-wheeling, dust cloud-spraying race of thought. It could be imagined as your brain's ability to improvise in thought. To navigate new ideas and constructs without a roadmap. Brainstorming is a good example of divergent thinking; you approach a new topic and quickly try and find the many disparate ideas that can be linked to it. These ideas themselves can then be linked together or lead to new spirals of interconnected thought and dialogue.

It is the "what if?", the "how about this...", the "Let's try this," type of approach.

This is the approach that we need to understand and practice if we are to achieve the lives of our dreams.

Chapter 11

Change

Around the 1800's in a cold and rainy England, something incredible was happening. Separately, across the country, people were creating new machines that could do the work of several men. A range of industries were shaken; textiles, metallurgy, tool manufacturing. The change came slowly at first, then all at once, and before England knew it the industrial revolution had arrived, coughing steam and coal and steel into the the roads and highways of the small island. People rushed to simply comprehend, then take advantage of the changes.

Like every revolution that preceded it those who were able to adapt their thinking fastest won. Sometimes big.

Those people who were best able to use divergent thinking and adapt to the unprecedented speed and level of change during the industrial revolution benefited far more than those stuck on convergent thinking, where the old paradigms and modalities were being thrown out day after day.

In fact, divergent thinkers didn't just benefit from the industrial revolution, they caused it. It took people like James Hargreaves, who invented and patented the *spinning jenny* in 1770. It was the first spinning frame of its kind, and introduced multiple spindles to the masses for an affordable price at only £6 in 1792. It could produce more, faster. A great combination for any product. The jenny was cheap too, made from a simple wooden frame attached to robust wooden mechanics, gears and pulleys. James Hargreaves had delivered something never seen before.

Across the country, James Watt, a mechanical engineer and chemist had collaborated with manufacturer Matthew Boulton to produce a new line of steam engines which James Watt had perfected. These were a precursor to the high-pressure steam engines of the 19th century which drove the trains and boats of the booming English empire.

These were people who used divergent thinking to come up with new solutions for problems that many people didn't even know existed. These people were analysts; they looked at their environment, saw a need and filled it. Their ideas form the backbone of the modern society so many enjoy today. Now we have Silicon Valley, the tourism culture and instant interconnectedness on a worldwide scale.

Men like James Watt and James Hargreaves were able to do what they did because they had a background in engineering, or science. Today however, those limitations do not apply. If there is something you wish to learn there are a staggering breadth and depth of articles, how-to's, videos and artwork to help you learn.

Going beyond that learning however, and entering divergent thinking, is up to you. Here are a few tips to get started.

Chapter 12

The Eight Attributes of Creativity

When we talk about divergent thinking, another paradigm we can use to look at it is the word creative. That is divergent thinking at its purest form. If we look then, to artists and creatives, what are the traits associated with creativity?

1. **Imagination:** The ability to think of multiple or related ideas.

2. **Flexibility:** The ability to think laterally across different categories when considering ideas.

3. **Elaboration:** The ability to add to or build on an   ideas.

4. **Originality:** The ability to create new and unique ideas.

5. **Complexity:** The ability to conceptualize complex ideas.

6. Risk Taking: The ability to be take risks on ideas.

7. Curiosity: The ability to ask and pose questions. The ability to listen and learn from the answers.

8. Fluency: The speed with which you can accomplish the above and move between the stages of creation.

Obviously it is not possible to have mastery of all eight attributes at all times, perfection is always out of reach for even the most talented humans. But if we can try and improve our skill in each of the areas we will find our divergent thinking grow stronger and more adaptable.

Every day, take a little time aside to hone in and practice each of these eight attributes. No matter what, we should always be writing down the ideas that come into our minds. Personally, I have an idea notebook where I write all of my ideas: **about 10 a day at minimum**. Once we implement this practice into our lives, after a few days and weeks, it begins to transform itself into a habitual behavior. We will find ourselves not having to force ideas into our minds, and they will be coming naturally to us throughout our day no matter what we are doing. What this does is it transforms our minds into idea creating machines, and when we are going about our day, seeing and experiencing different things, our minds will habitually create more and more ideas. Now, what we do with these ideas is all up to us. But nevertheless, ideas are **opportunities**. And maybe, just maybe, we'll grow the courage to turn these ideas into steps on our path toward success.

Part 3

LIVE

Wage the War on Resistance

Have you ever quit something more than once, started a new routine and never followed through, made a decision to make changes to your life and then gone back on your word... to yourself? About a year ago I received an invitation to join a fairly exclusive marketers forum from an acquaintance. While I was flattered and grateful for the offer, at that point in my life I didn't think I had the time to commit to it. I left it unread, and there it sat in my inbox, likely expired, probably useless. But still I couldn't quite get rid of it, nor open it and take the first steps to see if it would work or not. And so it lingered there, a daily reminder of my failure to follow through on my actions, a memo to myself that I had failed.

Sound familiar?

Why do we do these things to ourselves? Why do we make promises we don't keep to the person most important in our lives? (Hint: it's ourselves.) Steven

Pressfield calls this phenomenon *Resistance*; when our ego interferes with our actions out of fear. When we don't follow the path we know we must, and so contradict our very being with our actions leading to depression, anxiety and a sense of listlessness.

The problem is people are good at making up stories about themselves. Stories in the future, or stories in the past, or stories about the current situation. They'll say a man cut them off on the highway, which is why they're late, when they should have simply left earlier. They'll tell you their ex was a crazy person, when the reality is far more complex. They'll say that one day they hope to be successful, without ever defining what success means to them. They see soft-edged images of themselves succeeding and showing, once and for all, that they are just as brilliant as they think.

But all this is happening inside their head. Look out, externally, divergently, and see that facade drop away and reveal the world in all its splendor and drudgery. In their fantasy world, the person they want to become is so well defined and the road of how they're going to get there is so clear. Then you "wake up" and face resistance.

This is why so many people make promises to themselves in the evening; there's no chance of actually getting anything done and the mind is free to spin stories all night to satisfy your wanderlust. Then the cold light of morning arrives and suddenly accomplishing even one or two small tasks seems daunting.

It often comes in the form of excuses. You didn't sleep well, you've had an unexpected event occur, your dog is sick, the shower didn't work. You take it easy on yourself that day, bare minimum to get by. Then, by the evening, you're dreaming about the enormous obstacles you'll scale to the awe and amazement of friends and family. It sounds like a strange rhythm, yet many people play their life to it.

Pressfield writes that resistance is evil, toxic and the only reason we experience true unhappiness. He says we need to wage war on Resistance.

Chapter 13

Fear

This all comes from fear. When you decide you absolutely want a chocolate from the nearby gas station, you don't make excuses all day about what things have gotten in your way, how the stars didn't align *just* right for that Snickers to be in your mouth. You just go out and get it. If there's roadworks, you take a different route, if the gas station is closed, you walk to the next one. Maybe you get it, maybe you don't. Things happen, you handle it.

There is no fear of failure.

When you decide to go for promotion at work, or start a new career, or try anything that puts you outside of your comfort zone, you may experience a fear of failure. This is where resistance rears its ugly head.

But fear is good, it's a signal. Fear tells you that this thing *means something* to you. If it means something to you, then it's important, and if it's important, you can know that it's something you must do. In fact, the more fear when related to expressing yourself differently or changing your life, the more potential for growth. Therefore you should attend to it closely. If a task was worthless to our personal growth, we wouldn't care about it.

Understand it, Face it, Defeat it

Procrastination is another expression of resistance, as is self-sabotage in it's many forms. Resistance is more comfortable than reaching outside of our safe zone. First though, we must seek to understand its nature before we can face it and ultimately defeat it.

Pressfield says that the way we overcome Resistance is to change our mindset from an Amateur to that of a Pro. A Professional always does his work, he doesn't mind going the extra mile, he doesn't let small hiccups in his day throw him off track. So what does a Pro do differently than an Amatuer?

Chapter 14

The Pro and The Amateur

Patience and Persistence

Without a doubt, the level of patience and persistence one has determines the level of success and achievement they obtain in the future. As dreamers and achievers in the making, on our journey toward lasting and fulfilling success, we must understand that the route towards our desired destination will never be just one "straight-shot" road. There may be obstacles that fall on our path, challenges that demean our self-belief, and other roads that hinder our certainty. Therefore, we must understand that this "journey" is called a "journey" for a reason. It takes time, outstanding determination, and great amounts of pure effort; and although it seems difficult and mentally straining for us to consistently place so much effort on a single goal for a long period, this is exactly what we must do. We have to place effort every single day, even if it is the slightest bit, towards taking the next step in achieving our ultimate desire.

Success doesn't come in a day. It doesn't come in a week. It probably won't come in a month, and it may not come in a year. From the very beginning, this is something we must engrain in our minds so we do not fall short and give up hope too early. We must understand that everything in this world that is worth having takes time and effort to obtain. **Great** things take time. So unless we want to settle for the mediocre, achieve our very least, and unleash only a portion of our true potential, we must sacrifice the time and effort necessary to make the desire in our minds a physical part of our realities.

A Pro is patient. A Pro is always prepared to face extreme adversity and undergo enormous suffering in order to achieve a desired goal. Along with this, A pro is persistent. Giving up is never an option, and they remain in the "battle" and "fight" until they achieve what they aimed for from the beginning. However, Amateurs, like most people, lack these qualities. They want success and achievement in their lives, but they are never ready to give up what they must in order to receive what they want. They always want it the easy way. Naturally, an Amateur accepts defeat once the tough becomes a little too "tough."

Here is a short story about scientist and inventor Thomas Edison, who happened to see his own laboratory aflame:

In 1914 a fire broke out in Thomas Edison's laboratory. Machinery worth millions and all the papers pertaining to his lifelong research were burnt to ashes. Hearing of this tragedy his son Charles came looking for him and he found him standing by the side enjoying the leaping flames. On seeing Charles, Edison said to him: "Where is Your mother? Go find her and bring her here quickly; such a sight she will never see again!"

The next day, walking amidst the ashes of his hopes and dreams, the 67 year-old inventor said: "What benefit there is in destruction! All our mistakes have been burnt to ashes, thank God! Now we can begin afresh, all over again!

In reality, this story may or may not be true. But that's not the point. The point Is that this story contains the basis of truth about success, which is that success can only be achieved after tremendous amounts of effort and "trial-and-error." In truth, those who persist no matter the obstacles, who are ready to go against the winds of chance at any cost, sooner or later are bound to achieve success and fulfillment – no matter what.

Alongside this, this story also implies an important truth about success: one must come to fully embrace all failures. No matter the circumstance you are in, and regardless of what it is you are facing, it is you job to turn obstacles into stepping-stones, to transform negativity into positivity, to fully utilize your failures as tools for your own success. Indeed, every failure places you a few steps closer to succeeding; Every failure eliminates a wrong way, which brings you closer and closer towards finding the right way.

Along with this, a Pro...

- ✔ Seeks order of his physical and mental state. A pro takes care of their tools.
- Doesn't let fear inhibit his actions, ever. In fact for a Pro fear is a sign that they should pay attention and focus even more.
- Does not make excuses - When a Pro doesn't get what they want, they work on themselves and don't blame the external world.
- Is humble. A rich man doesn't have to tell you he's rich.
- Is prepared, like a boy scout a pro knows that luck is preparation meeting opportunity.
- Is continually learning. They will stop when they're dead.

- Never takes failure *or* success personally. The winds of chance can change direction at any time, the Pro is prepared for this, and knows that as long as they do their best they have nothing to regret.
- Faces and endures adversity, when things do go wrong as they inevitably will, a pro faces it with the same strength of character with which they faced everything else until now.
- Has a strong belief in themself.
- Doesn't live on autopilot - they pay attention to what happens around them and what they want to see, then make changes to themselves based on the difference.
- Takes risks. Calculated, rational and thoughtful ones. They handle their internal fear with deftness.

When you switch to the Pro mindset, Resistance become a signal to work harder, to pay attention. It defeats it completely.

Chapter 15

Proactive vs. Reactive

Don't let life control you; You control you.

We must try as Selfists to be proactive rather than reactive in our thinking and behavior.

Reactive people are at the mercy of the winds of change, they don't mentally plan or prepare; they simply react impulsively to whatever happens around them in the moment. They look externally, feel independently, think convergently and, as such, washed around in the frothy tides of life.

Proactive people on the other hand plan, prepare and adapt. When life throws them a curveball, they are not only expecting it, but prepared to "go with the flow" if it doesn't go as planned. Obviously, proactive people are going to have an easier time of it in general as they move through their lives.

What does this mean though, practically speaking?

Acceptance

"If you are distressed by anything external, the pain is not due to the thing itself, but to your estimate of it; and this you have the power to revoke at any moment." - Marcus Aurelius

First of all it means accepting that most things are outside of your control. Your boss is in a sour mood. Politicians are making harmful decisions. Your partner has left you. The grocery store is out of your favourite thing. Well, tough. These things are by and large outside of your control. If something is outside of your control, it is true madness to spend your limited time contemplating, talking about or otherwise worrying about it.

Of course, there's some actions you could take in these scenarios; you could make an honest effort to talk to your boss like a human and ask him how things are going. You could become more active politically. You can pick your next partner with more care. You could try another store or come earlier next time.

But, all of these things take effort. And as said before; we're good at making stories to suit our own narratives. My boss is an ass. Politicians are asses. My partner was an ass. The grocery stores is run by asses. Simpler, easier, and far more insidious than it may first appear.

The thing is, this is a huge paradigm shift for most people. Taking responsibility for one's own actions and to some degree their station in life is scary as all hell. Most people will resist at first, throwing up arguments and examples from their own life which justify their position.

But the truth is this: We are in control. If we choose to be.

We don't have to be influenced by unpredictable events or the negative emotions of others.

"Everything can be taken from a man but one thing: the last of the human freedoms- to choose one's attitude in any given set of circumstances, to choose one's own way." – Viktor Frankl, Holocaust survivor.

When we are proactive, we concern ourselves solely with the things that are inside our circle of influence, rather than worrying about things we cannot do anything about. We look towards what we are able to control and change, including the way we react to any given situation. If the grocery stores is out of that really important thing for the birthday cake we're making, we don't get upset at something we can't change, we change ourselves or our plans. In this case, we go to another grocery store and make a mental note to ring the store beforehand next time before we leave.

Likewise, we can't alter the way someone else behaves or talks to us. We can only change how we react to that behaviour.

We have no control over the weather. But, we can always choose our thought process, and our responses. So we can check the report before leaving the house and dress accordingly, or keep a raincoat in the car.

Being proactive is not about being a robot or having no emotions. Rather, it's being in control of your emotions and recognising that losing your internal calm because of something outside of your control is madness. It's making the transition from other things being in charge of your life and emotions, to being in charge of yourself.

Instead of shifting the blame elsewhere, you can begin to carry the responsibility of your own mistakes. If all the other grocery stores are closed and the party is in three hours, most people will get upset at the grocery store, when they should be upset at themselves for not taking any number of steps that would have ensured they had all the necessary ingredients on time. You cease the habit of expecting external circumstances to change to suit you, and instead alter yourself internally.

Conclusion

I hope it's clear to you by now that there is only one person for you to hold accountable for your success or failure: **you**. Not many people see the world through that lens, why?

It's hard. It's hard to accept that you bear the full weight of many of the negative things that happen to you. It's easier to accept the responsibility only for the good, and spin stories about the wicked world working against you when things don't go your way. I'm not suggesting that bad things won't happen, nor am I suggesting that you can stop all of those things from happening. But what you can do is be *prepared* for the changes and trials that life will inevitably throw at you. You can shoulder them with grace and not allow them to throw you off-course of your goal.

The components that make up a successful mindset are not limited to those I have written about here, there are more, many more. Part of that mindset is seeking others who share your perspective, or better yet, those who *challenge* it. Seek new knowledge, test it, throw out what doesn't work, keep what does.

Remember too that failure is an integral part of success, if you are trying your best, you should be failing sometimes, that's normal, it builds your character and resilience, it can teach you gratitude. Life will constantly hand you lessons, pay attention to them. Tenacity breeds success. Keep striving, keep moving.

I wish the best of luck.

Afterword:

If you enjoyed this book, you might enjoy these relevant selections I have written:

Click:

Million Dollar Habits: 27 Powerful Habits to Wire

Your Mind for Success, Become Truly Happy, and

Achieve Financial Freedom

The Art of Belief: Design Your Mind to Destroy

Limitations, Unleash Your Inner-Greatness, and

Achieve the Success of Your Dreams

Made in the USA
Lexington, KY
24 August 2017